Cover photograph
An aerial view of Ludlow (Shropshire)
from the south
(Photograph: Trevor Rowley.)

British Library Cataloguing in Publication Data
Haslam, Jeremy
Early medieval towns in Britain. — (Shire archaeology; 45)
1. Cities and towns, Medieval — Great Britain
I. Title
941'.009'732 HT133
ISBN 0-85263-758-6

Published by
SHIRE PUBLICATIONS LTD
Cromwell House, Church Street, Princes Risborough,
Aylesbury, Bucks HP17 9AJ, UK.

Series Editor: James Dyer

ISBN 0 85263 758 6

First published 1985

Set in 11 point Times and printed in Great Britain by
C. I. Thomas & Sons (Haverfordwest) Ltd,
Press Buildings, Merlins Bridge, Haverfordwest, Dyfed.

Contents

List of illustrations

Acknowledgements

I acknowledge with gratitude the people who have helped me in the production of this book. Photographs and drawings have been kindly supplied by Martin Biddle (Winchester), Cambridge University (Sudbury), Tony Dyson (London), Simon Griffin and Mark Brisbane (Southampton), Richard Hall (York), Carolyn Heighway (Gloucester), Tim Tatton-Brown (Canterbury), and Wiltshire County Council (Cricklade). Trevor Rowley has generously made available his slide of the aerial view of Ludlow (front cover), and assisted in other ways. Finally my wife Claudia has compiled the index, and also assisted with support and encouragement.

1
Introduction

This book gives a short account of some of the physical evidence for urban development from the end of the Roman period until about AD 1140. The question of the development of town life, though, is a matter for wider debate, embracing evidence from historical and numismatic sources, but also increasingly (as it is hoped to show in the following pages) evidence from archaeological and topographical sources. Life in towns is, however, lived within the fabric of the townscape, and each determines in complex ways the quality or form of the other. An account therefore of some of the topographical and archaeological evidence relating to the development of the townscape is desirable insofar as it contributes evidence and hypotheses to this broader enquiry.

The method of presentation used in this book attempts to set the physical evidence within a historical framework describing the course of development of towns. In many places this framework has itself had to be presented as a series of historical hypotheses which seem to the author best to accommodate all the available evidence. These are put forward not as statements of a currently agreed position (such a situation does not, and perhaps should not, exist) but rather as conceptual models which can be tested by further analysis and synthesis. In following this procedure it has been necessary to go against many apparently established 'truths' (in particular about the development of burhs from the late eighth century to the early tenth) and go beyond what many would regard as the limits of legitimate speculation.

The account is restricted to brief descriptions and discussions of the physical evidence, of which comparative topographical analysis is a major and hitherto undervalued historical resource. This has necessitated the omission of discussions of more theoretical and general aspects, such as the nature of urban development, the nature and extent of redistributive or market exchange mechanisms as they affect pre-urban, proto-urban or fully urban settlements, and the wider considerations of towns within the total landscape. Nor are details given, except in passing, about the value of artefacts from excavations, about building types, the arrangement of houses within plots, the structural development of churches and their spatial evolution within the townscape, or the layout and development of waterfront structures. The study of these and other details will, when properly assessed, contribute enormously to a total picture of the development both of urban places and of urban life.

Even though the nature of urban settlements is not discussed, it is necessary here to emphasise the need for historical relevance in their study. Though objective criteria have been put forward to establish whether a place is urban or not, it is important to consider whether these are relevant for earlier — and indeed later — periods. There is the danger that the absence of such criteria might be taken to imply that a place was not urban at any period. A settlement growing up around a royal and/or ecclesiastical site in the seventh or eighth century should not be judged as non-urban by the criteria applicable to a later Saxon burh, just as these latter places should not be judged by the standards of later medieval market towns. The smaller, less developed settlements may have been as 'urban' to the surrounding contemporary population as the later ones clearly were. In short, each place, at any period in its history, must be assessed by the standards of its own time rather than of any other.

2
The Roman heritage

It is generally accepted that urban life in Roman times disappeared everywhere in the course of the fifth century. This process of disintegration was the result of a decline in the fourth century; as a consequence of the end of the military presence and the disappearance both of a stable coinage and of organised industrial production. For similar reasons the cities of the Incas, whose functioning was dependent upon a complex state administrative system, were rapidly abandoned when the Spanish conquest led to the break-up of that system in the sixteenth century. The earlier idea that the disappearance of the Roman urban order was the result of destructive inroads by Saxon settlers has long been abandoned. However, without the former existence of Roman towns and the survival of many of the physical elements of the Roman landscape into later centuries (for instance town defences, stone buildings, roads, and estates and their boundaries), and also some social and religious elements, both the geography and the whole course of development of the succeeding Saxon centuries would probably have been unrecognisably different.

There is general agreement for the existence of a fundamental break in 'urban' life in Britain in the fifth century, if not earlier. Towns differing in function, siting and physical and social organisation developed anew in the Saxon period to reflect a changed society. The question of 'continuity' between Roman and Saxon must be discussed therefore not in terms of survival of towns as social organisms but in other less direct ways. Two of these can be discussed here.

Firstly, the physical elements of Roman townscapes such as defences and gates, some streets and stone buildings, can be shown in many instances to have survived into periods when they influenced both the siting and indeed some details of the layout of later Saxon towns. In many former Roman towns the survival and continued use of gates in the defences has caused the main streets of the later town to follow the alignment of the Roman streets between these gates. Other examples of such physical continuity are mentioned below. Conversely, the loss of these elements, in particular street alignments, in the post-Roman period is usually taken as evidence for the loss of their function.

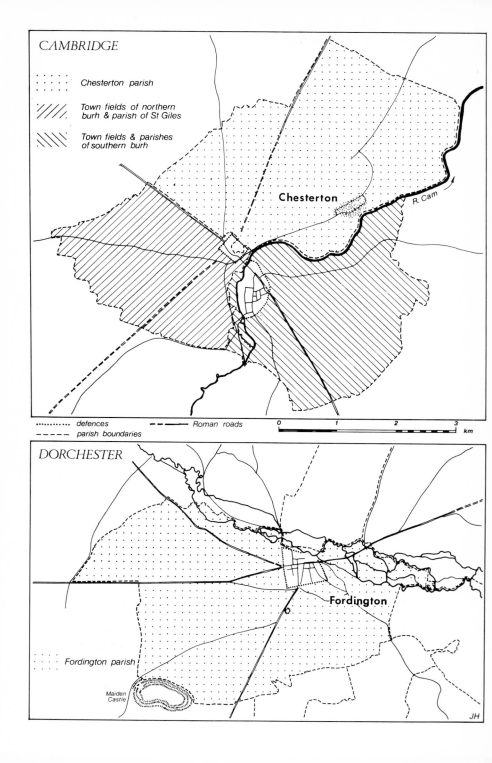

CAMBRIDGE

· · · · · · · Chesterton parish

/////. Town fields of northern
burh & parish of St Giles

\\\\\ Town fields & parishes
of southern burh

Chesterton

R. Cam

·········· defences   ----- Roman roads
----- parish boundaries

0   1   2   3
                                    km

DORCHESTER

Fordington

· · · · · Fordington parish

Maiden
Castle

JH

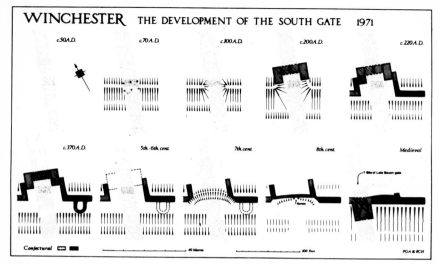

WINCHESTER THE DEVELOPMENT OF THE SOUTH GATE 1971

Fig. 2. Winchester: the development of the south gate, showing stages of modification of the Roman gateway throughout the Saxon period. (Winchester Excavations Committee.)

Fig. 1. FACING PAGE: Parishes surrounding Cambridge and Dorchester (Dorset), which probably comprise the former Roman *territoria*.

Secondly, and in many ways more importantly, it seems likely that Roman towns of all sizes provided centres for the organisation of such local and regional administration as the Saxon or British successors to the Roman order were able to maintain. In many instances they also survived as religious (i.e. Christian) centres. Since, as will become apparent, the increasing number of urban or proto-urban places recognisable from about AD 700 were both administrative and ecclesiastical centres, these factors are of some importance.

The continuation of many Roman towns as 'centres of authority' into later centuries is highly significant. The defences of some of these, such as Winchester and possibly London and Canterbury, were refurbished during this early period (fig. 2). The defeat of kings in Gloucester, Cirencester and Bath in 571 by incoming Saxons shows that each town was then the administrative centre of a small kingdom. Similarly, both London and Canterbury remained as central refuges for kingdoms or tribes in the fifth and sixth centuries; a royal palace certainly existed at London from the early seventh century, if not earlier. It seems likely that such places emerged as non-urban centres of royal authority by possibly continuous development from the Roman period. Furthermore, in many cases it is very probable that the territories attached to the former Roman centres have been perpetuated in later parish and other boundaries. Such estates can be reconstructed around for instance Winchester, Chichester, Gloucester, Cirencester and Dorchester in southern England, and Great Casterton, Cambridge and Godmanchester and others in the Midlands (fig. 1).

A different though related series of developments can be detected in the establishment of royal vills in the early or middle Saxon period as the centres of large estates or territories in close topographical relationship to former Roman towns. This process seems to have occurred widely over much of lowland England at many different levels (though at precisely what period is not clear) and implies that such centres show some functional continuity with earlier ones. In the west of England this development seems to have often occurred as the stage after a shift of the regional centre to a redefended hillfort. Such shifts of focus can be recognised for instance from *Sorviodunum* (Roman Salisbury) to Wilton, *Cunetio* to Ramsbury, Ilchester to Somerton, Wickham to Winchcombe, Great Casterton to Stamford, Caistor-by-Norwich to possibly Thorpe near Norwich, Duston to Northampton, Kenchester to Hereford, Dorchester (Dorset) to Fordington, and Cambridge to Chesterton. In the last two examples these places became the centres of territories which encircled the former Roman town, from which areas the later town parishes were carved out (fig. 1). Since, as will be seen, the numerous small towns of later centuries were to develop in their turn in close relationship to these early royal centres, these developments provide vital links between the Roman period and the fully developed urban landscape of the late Saxon period.

Evidence of ecclesiastical continuity from Roman towns to later priods is intriguing, but in England perhaps less relevant to subsequent urban developments than on the continent. The survival of a Christian population through the fifth and sixth centuries can in several places begin to be demonstrated from archaeological evidence. In Exeter the old forum area became the burial area for the sub-Roman Christian community, surviving as the precincts of an early monastery and minster church, later the new minster of the early tenth century and the Norman cathedral. A similar development has recently been demonstrated at Lincoln, where the church of St Paul-in-the-

Bail, built by Paulinus in the early seventh century, was placed symmetrically in relation to a presumably still standing forum, which had already been used in the fifth and sixth centuries as a burial ground. A parallel case may exist in London, where a possibly late Roman church (St Peter's) appears to have survived within the basilica of the forum, and there is also good evidence for the survival of a Christian population at Canterbury. All these instances, however, imply continuity of population, and perhaps local administration, rather than of urban function.

A related series of developments is the metamorphosis into churches of Christian martyr tombs situated in extramural Roman cemeteries, which would have attracted local settlement. Examples can be seen at London and Ilchester (churches of St Andrew), Godmanchester (St Mary's) (fig. 5) and Canterbury (St Martin's and possibly other churches). At both Wells and St Albans, however, this process led by a rather indirect route to the foundation of new towns at these places in later periods. On the continent this common process often resulted in the shift of focus of the later urban centre around this church and away from the site of the former Roman town, though in England this process seems to have happened infrequently if at all.

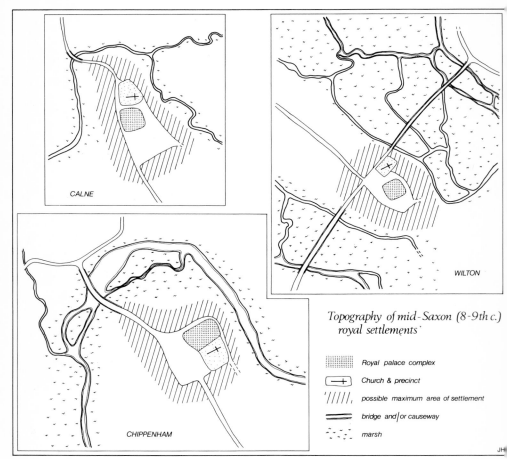

Fig. 3. Reconstructed topography of some middle Saxon royal settlements in Wiltshire.

3
Middle Saxon towns

During the seventh century the first glimmerings of the establishment of at least the basis of a new urban order can be discerned.
There are perhaps two main directions which were to be taken in
these formative stages of urban growth: firstly, the gradual
development of specialised functions — economic, social and
ecclesiastical — of settlements at or closely related to royal estate
and administrative centres, including many former Roman towns;
and secondly, the foundation of new coastal or estuarine towns in
southern and eastern England as trading centres under royal
protection.

The royal estate centres of the middle Saxon period were the
instruments by which much of England was administered.
Through them the considerable resources of the landscape were
utilised, and probably actively organised, by the king and his
agents. They must have functioned as centres of production of
agricultural produce and other goods and of the local, if not also
regional, exchange of these; they became furthermore the sites of
minster churches, to which tithes were paid. Their specialised
administrative, religious, economic and ceremonial functions
must to contemporaries have set them apart from purely rural
settlements. These considerations, the possibility mentioned
above of some functional continuity of these places with Roman
settlements and the fact that many of these centres, in particular
in southern England, developed in later centuries into recognisable and reasonably well documented towns suggest that they can
be described as 'proto-urban' places (they have already been
described by some as 'significant places' or 'primary towns'). This
description carries the implication that from an early period these
settlements possessed specialised characteristics which are recognisable in developed form at a later date. The apparently
'organic' metamorphosis of these early royal sites into towns in
the tenth and eleventh centuries appears, however, to have been
inhibited in the Midlands by the creation of large burhs on new
sites as administrative and trading centres in the late eighth and
tenth centuries, an effect which can also be recognised around
large burhs in the south such as Winchester and London.

These places can be recognised as a widespread phenomenon
by the early eighth century and may well have had earlier roots in

Plate 1. Canterbury: huts of the late sixth to early seventh century at 16 Watling Street (1978). In the background a deeply sunken hut of the seventh century cuts an earlier and shallower hut. (Photograph: Kevin Blockley, Canterbury Archaeological Trust.)

the seventh or even the sixth century. It seems probable that the present day topography of three of these settlements in Wiltshire (Calne, Chippenham and Wilton) preserves a layout which may well be middle Saxon in origin (fig. 3). These (and other) places are generally located on characteristic sites, occupying positions combining local inaccessibility with regional accessibility, which suggests an origin as planted settlements. In these three instances an open area (with possible original market and/or ceremonial function) is associated with both an early minster church site and an area indicated by place-name evidence (e.g. 'Kingsbury') as being the site of a small enclosure, probably containing the royal residence. Around these topographical elements settlement either grew or was laid out, forming the nucleus of the later town.

It is very probable that the central ecclesiastical role of these places was as much an incentive to urban development as was their role as royal estate centres. Excavations at Canterbury have shown a burgeoning of settlement of apparently unorganised form within the former defences from the late sixth century which can be directly attributed to the new ecclesiastical presence established by St Augustine (plate 1). The growth of important monastic centres such as Malmesbury or Glastonbury in the seventh and eighth centuries must also have attracted relatively large settlements of at least proto-urban character, as they certainly appear to have done in contemporary Ireland.

Some recent arguments have suggested that the development of these proto-urban places as towns was either consequent upon the replacement of a redistributive economy by a true 'market' economy with the building of burhs in the early tenth century or, alternatively, the result of a policy on the part of later Saxon kings of 'founding' towns on their estates to augment their revenues. These hypotheses do not, however, provide adequate explanations for the demonstrable (but not quantifiable) multi-functional roles of these centres from a considerably earlier period.

In contrast to these small proto-urban places at royal or ecclesiastical centres, the period from the early seventh century onwards saw the rise of a number of comparatively large trading settlements on coastal locations in southern and eastern England, which developed in response to the growth of trading activities involving northern Europe as a whole. These places, most of them on new sites, were often called *'-wics'* and included York *(Eoforwiceastor)*, Norwich, Fordwich, Ipswich, London *(Lundenwic)*, Sandwich and Southampton *(Hamwic)*. They developed in parallel with other similar sites from Scandinavia to France, such as Ribe, Haithabu, Dorestadt and Quentavic. Each of these places appears to have been connected with an important royal centre, for instance Ipswich with Rendlesham, Dunwich with Blythburgh, Sandwich and Fordwich with Canterbury, and *Hamwic* with Winchester, suggesting that they were 'ports of trade' for a kingdom, founded by royal initiative as the means by which foreign trade could be brought under direct royal control. The development of inland centres at the borders of kingdoms, such as Cambridge (between Mercia and East Anglia), and the royal interest in the salt-producing *'-wics'* (Droitwich and Nantwich) seem to have been part of the same phenomenon.

Of these trading centres, London is perhaps the most fully documented from historical evidence. Probably from the early seventh century, if not rather earlier, it combined within its

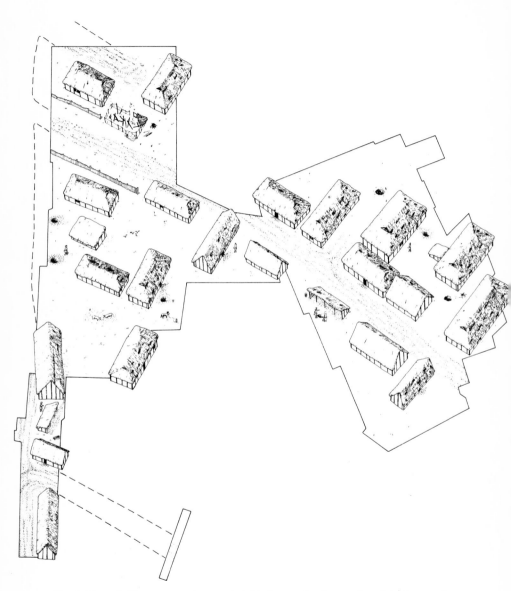

Fig. 4. *Hamwic* (Southampton): an artist's bird's-eye view impression of the layout of part of the middle Saxon town, based on excavated evidence at the Seven Dials site. (Drawing by Simon Griffin. Copyright, Southampton Museums Service.)

former Roman defences the functions of a royal and ecclesiastical centre on its western side and a commercial port and trading settlement on its eastern side. These functions were similarly combined at York. Each of these areas at London appears to have been served by a street market, Westcheap and Eastcheap, both of which have some claim to continuity of use from Roman streets. It was probably an outport for the Mercian kingdom from the early eighth century, and its position at the borders of several kingdoms (Essex, Kent, Mercia and Wessex), as well as its proximity to the continent, must have ensured its success as a settlement and trading port. The evidence suggests that after a period of near desertion from the later fifth to the late sixth century the extent of settlement in at least parts of London would have grown rapidly to the point where it once again would have become by the standards of the time a truly urban place.

The most fully documented of these places from an archaeological point of view is *Hamwic*. A number of excavations have demonstrated the existence of a settlement, on a flat estuarine site to the east of the present Southampton, covering at least 45 hectares (111 acres), with a sub-rectilinear system of gravel-surfaced streets. Fronting on to these streets were timber-framed and wattle houses set within their own fenced properties, each of which also included pits, latrines, wells and outbuildings (fig. 4). This and other evidence suggests that the settlement was probably initiated by King Ine (688 - 726) and laid out and perhaps maintained by continuing royal authority. It is also possible that in the seventh century a colony of northern European merchants lived, and were buried, on the site before the formal layout of the town. Excavations have shown that the town grew rapidly in the first four decades of the eighth century and experienced another boom in the late eighth and early ninth centuries, and that for much of this time it must have acted as an outport for Mercia as well as Wessex. Its inhabitants, as well as including foreign merchants, comprised specialised craft workers engaged in bone working and iron smithing, amongst other activities. The numerous bone finds, furthermore, show that the town was supported by the efficient exploitation of the well organised agricultural resources of the surrounding region, with animals being brought to the town on the hoof. It is probable that the later destruction of this agricultural support system by the Vikings in the 840s would have been an important factor in the demise of the town.

While the growth of places such as Ipswich and *Hamwic* was

not the result of a free internal market economy, the development of the small inland royal centres as proto-urban places in the
middle Saxon period carries the implication, contrary to recent
suggestions, that these forces were operating on a small scale in
the middle Saxon period. The existence of this internal trading
network provides a context for the emergence of such places as
Cambridge and Northampton as regional centres of exchange
(though not necessarily as organised urban settlements), for the
reform of the coinage in the late eighth century and, it is
suggested in the next section, for the development of the first
urban burhs by King Offa at this same period.

4
The development of burhs: eighth to early ninth century

The Anglo-Saxon word _burh_ means a fortified enclosure and may refer either to a small private plot, such as the enclosure around a royal or thegnly residence, or to a larger public fortress. Public fortresses, of all shapes and sizes, were established usually against Viking aggression on many different types of site. Many of these, on hilltops or naturally inaccessible spur sites, were clearly defended only by an impermanent garrison. The larger ones on flatter sites or larger spur sites would however have been defended settlements, the construction and upkeep of their defences and their general military effectiveness guaranteed by a permanent population which in most if not all cases must have been urban in character.

There is some evidence for the hypothesis that in the late eighth century King Offa established a series of such public burhs in Mercia as a systematic and comprehensive defence of his kingdom against Viking attack, which began at this time. These were large defended places which in the main were sited to block penetration by Viking warships up the major estuaries and rivers of both western and eastern Mercia, and it seems probable that these burhs formed part of a defensive system which included Offa's Dyke on the western edge of the kingdom. It can be suggested that they included Hereford, Winchcombe, Oxford, Northampton, Bedford, Cambridge (fig. 5), Tamworth, Stamford, Nottingham, London, Godmanchester, Leicester, Lincoln, Chester, and possibly also Worcester, Norwich and Canterbury. All of these places were already by the later eighth century important royal and/or ecclesiastical centres. Some of them were former Roman towns whose probably still standing defences would have been reutilised. Eight of these, possibly ten — Hereford, Winchcombe, Oxford, Northampton, Bedford, Tamworth, Nottingham, Stamford, and possibly Worcester and Norwich — were, however, new burhs on sites developed since the Roman period, whose defences and internal street system were generally laid out on a more or less rectilinear plan, and whose comparatively large size suggests that they were also new urban foundations (for Bedford see fig. 5). They were all, furthermore, closely associated with a bridge or bridges over a major river, both burh and bridge forming a single military unit designed to control movement both across and along these rivers. The construction of these places at the same time as the reform of the coinage suggests that they were set up as fortified trading centres, those on the eastern side of England functioning probably as inland ports for North Sea trade. Other considerations suggest that the initiation of this system was accompanied by the creation of new shires, of which the burhs were intended to be the military, administrative and economic centres. It is further possible that Tamworth, the 'capital' of the Mercian kingdom, was constructed as a defended urban centre half a century earlier in the reign of Aethelbald.

Archaeological and topographical work is helping to elucidate the character of many of these places. The earliest defences of Oxford, Tamworth, Hereford, Winchcombe and Nottingham can be dated to the middle Saxon period (i.e. before about 850); at Hereford and Bedford it appears that these defences were laid out over a large spreading settlement already in existence. A defended enclosure at Norwich, its origin as yet undated but probably belonging to the same Mercian system of the late eighth century, was established around an early east-west routeway of Roman origin at a river bridging point. It appears to have succeeded a settlement with a number of centres in the immediate area and which acted as an early trading settlement or '-*wic*', in this respect showing some similarities to the Mercian burh at Cambridge. At Oxford the long causeway across the Thames valley to its south, presumably associated with one or more bridges, has been demonstrated by excavation to have been newly constructed at precisely the period — the late eighth century — to which the construction of this defensive system can be assigned. Here, as in other places, the main streets, bridge or bridges, causeway and defences were most likely laid out in one operation.

Together with these features it is possible that areas of the surrounding land, usually a royal estate, were made over to the burh inhabitants as the 'town fields'. This land would in most cases have been coterminous with, or a part of, the area of the church parish of the burh. This pattern can certainly be recognised at Cambridge, where the fields of the northern town (and Mercian burh) occupy the same area as its parish (St Giles) (fig. 1). The pattern of parishes of the northern (Mercian) burh at Bedford shows clearly how the parishes of the burh churches

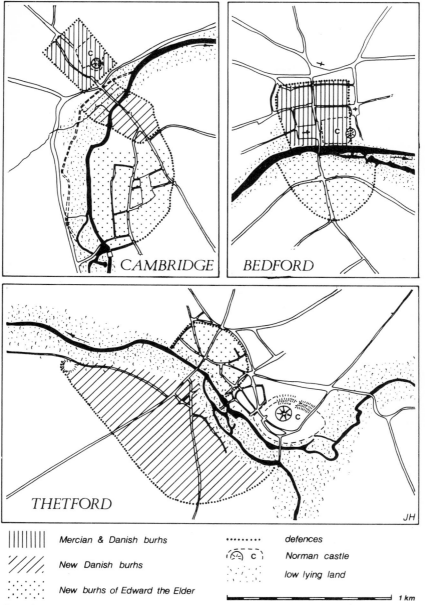

Fig. 5. Successive Mercian, Danish and Edwardian (early tenth-century) defended settlements at Cambridge, Bedford and Thetford (Norfolk).

(initially probably one parish) have been carved out of those of surrounding villages. In like manner, many of the mills associated with these burhs may have been royal endowments to the inhabitants on the foundation of the burh; such indeed may have been the function of the remarkable eighth-century mill discovered at Tamworth immediately outside one of the original gates. A similar pattern of the association of burh, fields and mill can be recognised in some of the early tenth-century burhs discussed below.

The details of the internal layout of these burhs are at present largely unknown. Most of the side streets of the later towns appear to have been additions to the main streets, as in the case of Oxford in the early tenth century. Some side streets in Lincoln were laid out during the Viking occupation in the later ninth century. That an intramural or 'wall' street around the inner edge of the defences formed one element in the layout of these burhs is suggested by evidence of the addition of this street to the Roman defences of Chester at probably this period, and by topographical indications of a similar feature at a number of places, such as Hereford, Northampton, Bedford and Oxford. In Cambridge small enclosures of the middle Saxon period lay within the defences, and at Bedford the alignments of timber structures of the same period appear to have borne some relation to the original street pattern. Elsewhere, however, evidence of the layout of properties is slight, though there are some indications that their arrangement would have been comparatively irregular, with houses dispersed within relatively spacious enclosures or *hagae*. This pattern can be detected in parts of middle Saxon London and at Winchester before the period of Alfredian restoration in the late ninth century, as well as in Northampton in the late ninth and early tenth centuries. One of these enclosures in the late eighth and ninth centuries at Winchester (Fig. 6), in the area of medieval Tanner Street (Brook Street), comprised both a double-roomed two-storeyed masonry building as well as timber buildings. This structural complex reused parts of a surviving Roman building, with the stone building possibly acting as a secure structure for the working of precious metals. In both London and Canterbury, however, both dispersed properties and relatively dense housing fronting on to streets appear to have existed within the defences at an early date.

While these few details are similar in many respects to those of purely rural settlements, it should not be concluded that these burhs were not urban. The urban status of a place at this period

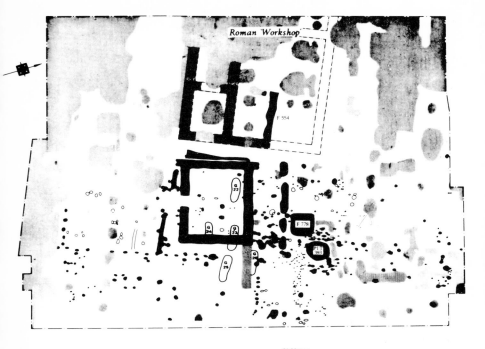

ECH

Fig. 6. Winchester: Lower Brook Street, levels and features of the eighth and ninth centuries. (Winchester Excavation Committee.)

(as at any other) was determined as much by its function as by its morphology. From the beginning these places may well have acted as regional market centres. A common feature of their layout is a large extramural market area, usually associated with an early church, outside one of the gates. Such a feature can be recognised for instance at Oxford, Hereford, Nottingham, Stamford, Bedford (Fig. 5), Northampton and London (Smithfield). The positions of most of these burhs at generally the lowest crossing points of rivers would have made them ideally suitable sites for North Sea trade. Some indication of foreign contacts is given by a pottery industry at Stamford in the mid ninth century showing influences from the Rhineland and northern France, as well as by the distribution of finds of middle Saxon lava querns in eastern England, which are concentrated on sites along the major rivers.

The paucity of evidence of much formal internal layout of these burhs, apart from main streets, wall streets and defences, could possibly be explained by suggesting that their performances as urban places did not live up to the expectations of their royal founder. Social instability arising from the political crises within Mercia after Offa's death and the eventual expansion and ascendency of Wessex in the ninth century, together with increasing Viking raiding, could hardly have encouraged urban expansion in Mercia after the early ninth century. Their fortunes may indeed have been exactly mirrored by that of *Hamwic,* which, after a period of prosperity in the late eighth and early ninth centuries, declined until its at least partial demise soon after and probably as a consequence of Viking raiding in the 840s.

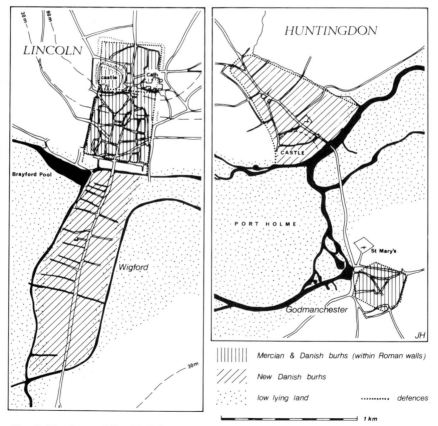

Fig. 7. Mercian and Danish defended settlements, the former within Roman walls, the latter built around Roman or Mercian roads and bridges.

5
Viking towns:
late ninth to early tenth century

Though Viking depredations in the middle of the ninth century probably caused widespread de-urbanisation in northern Europe, it is now becoming increasingly clear that it was the Vikings themselves who were responsible for the transformation of urban life in England, as elsewhere in northern Europe, in the half century 875-925.

It appears that the Viking armies occupied the former Mercian burhs, and the associated shires of those in at least eastern Mercia became the territories administered by each division of the army. Recent archaeological and topographical research has suggested that in their wake civilian trading settlements grew up, developments which can be recognised not only in the larger centres such as York and Lincoln but also in the smaller places such as Huntingdon, Cambridge, Stamford and Norwich. This evidence suggests that the presence of the Vikings, with their access to Scandinavian, European and Asian markets, and their advanced nautical and shipbuilding techniques, was from the later ninth century the motivating force for a phase of unprecedented urban expansion.

In many instances the Danish trading places, as well as colonising earlier fortifications, developed as new and characteristic urban extensions which were in many cases provided with their own defences. These can be recognised at York, Lincoln, Nottingham, Stamford, Huntingdon, Cambridge, Norwich, Thetford, Ipswich, London and perhaps Southwark. They came to form separate urban nuclei of a distinctive but hitherto unrecognised topographical type, which show common characteristics: they usually developed as linear settlements on low-lying ground along existing routeways leading to earlier centres, many of them at bridging points of major rivers. All of them occupied areas with easy access to river and estuarine navigation.

The most dramatic examples of this topographical type are perhaps Wigford, the southern 'suburb' of Lincoln, and Huntingdon (fig. 7). Both developed along Roman roads approaching earlier centres (Lincoln and Godmanchester respectively) which were arguably utilised as Mercian burhs and which must have acted as the initial Danish army bases. Wigford was associated

Plate 2. York: Viking houses of the early tenth century, made of timber and wattle, fronting on to Coppergate (to left). (Photograph: York Archaeological Trust.)

with the harbour of Brayford Pool (then somewhat larger than now) and was accessible by both river and canal from both the Humber estuary (via the Trent) and the Wash (via the Witham). Huntingdon shows a similar dependence on river navigation; it was certainly fortified by the Danes and was arguably created by them as a new urban foundation or inland port in the last quarter of the ninth century. A similar though smaller burh developed along the Roman road south of the river at Cambridge (fig. 5). In these and other examples such as York (discussed below) the topography suggests a controlled development of the trading area by long contiguous properties with houses fronting the street, and in the case of Wigford and Cambridge with possibly warehouses and wharves at the ditches or canals to the rear. This pattern is attested archaeologically at York. A similar topographical development along the Roman road approaching London Bridge at Southwark suggests the possibility that this area was, like Wigford, a Danish trading settlement.

In a number of towns these areas are associated with a parish church of St Clement, a favourite Danish dedication. The defended Danish burh at Cambridge was until the early twelfth century nearly coterminous with the parish of St Clement; and a large enclosure to the north of an early bridge at Norwich, whose

Plate 3. York: Viking houses of the mid tenth century, to the rear of those shown in plate 2 and occupying contiguous properties. Timber upright holding boards line sunken 'cellars', which probably functioned as workshops. (Photograph: York Archaeological Trust.)

defences are late ninth-century in origin, has a St Clement's church as its central church. Other parishes of St Clement occupy low-lying areas around early routeways near a river at Ipswich and London (St Clement Danes), both of which were centres of Danish settlement and commerce. Similar parishes occur for instance at Sandwich, Old Romney and Hastings, suggesting a proliferation in the decades around 900 of small centres at convenient coastal locations. The Danish army bases at, for instance, Reading and Wareham may also have developed into similar trading settlements. Surprisingly, a St Clement's parish is also situated around the western end of an early (probably Roman and Mercian) bridgehead at Worcester, suggesting the presence of a Hiberno-Norse trading settlement using the river Severn for trade between western Mercia and Ireland.

These topographical hypotheses are to a great extent validated by the results of recent archaeological work, in particular in York and Lincoln. At both of these places it has been demonstrated that the Viking presence led to rapid urban expansion. At York the Anglian royal, trading and ecclesiastical centre within the Roman fortress was transformed in the late ninth century by the growth of a Viking trading settlement to the south-east between the two rivers. This shift must have been encouraged, as at Lincoln and most other places already mentioned, by the greater accessibility of the area to water transport. This involved the replacement of the Roman bridge over the Ouse by a new bridge leading along Ousegate to the heart of this settlement, the planning of streets and the laying out of long narrow properties along them, the construction of wharves on both the rivers Ouse and Foss and the refurbishment of the defences. At Coppergate the property boundaries were established around 900, surviving virtually unchanged until the present. They were occupied by timber houses set gable-end to the street within regularly laid-out properties marked by fences (plate 2), with similar buildings at the rear of the properties near the river. It seems probable that these latter were warehouses which would have received goods unloaded from boats and destined to be worked in and sold from the house-shops on the street front. In the decade 950-60 the earlier houses were replaced, within the original properties, by more substantial sunken houses with walls of pegged oak uprights lined with planks (plate 3), whose regular layout and construction suggest the operation of some form of civic planning authority at this period. Various domestic industries were carried out in this area, such as glassmaking (in the ninth century), metalworking

Plate 4. York: wooden bowls of the Viking period, made in the workshops shown in plate 3. (Photograph: York Archaeological Trust.)

Plate 5. York: bone combs of the Viking period, also made at the Coppergate site. (Photograph: York Archaeological Trust.)

(lead, bronze, silver and gold), die-cutting and coin production, and the working of bone and antler, amber, jet, wood and leather (plates 4 and 5). Finds of domestic and other material of this period along Walmgate, a probable early approach road to the south-eastern side of the Roman fortress, suggest contemporary development, possibly within defences, along this street as well. This is significant in that this area is topographically very similar to the suggested Viking trading areas at other centres already mentioned.

The picture of at least the central parts of York in the late ninth and early tenth centuries is therefore one of dense, squalid yet vibrant and creative urban life, relying on the wide trading contacts of the Vikings. There is evidence that this must have been typical, if not in degree then certainly in kind, of many of the places previously discussed. At Lincoln, a phase of planning in the lower *colonia,* involving the layout of at least one new street and buildings fronting on to it, can be attributed to the Viking presence in the late ninth century. At Stamford widespread Viking settlement and an associated iron-smelting industry have been recognised within the outer ring of defences, for whose origin in the Viking period there is strong inferential evidence. Similarly at Thetford a large and spreading urban settlement with planned streets and regular properties laid along them has been excavated to the south of the present town, again enclosed by defences probably of Viking origin (fig. 5). Even as far inland as Northampton there is growing evidence of a period of urban renewal and growth subsequent to, and consequent upon, the use of the suggested Mercian burh as a Danish army base.

Similar developments can be recognised in many places in Ireland. Towns of similar topographical type to the English ones described above were established at several sites around the coast by the Vikings, all of them in existence by the later ninth century, and arguably by then well developed as urban places which must have had trading contacts with the towns on the western side of England. These include (from west to east) Limerick, Cork, Youghal, Waterford, Wexford and Dublin.

The evidence suggests, therefore, that a period of widespread re-urbanisation at many earlier centres, after faltering Mercian beginnings, was one of the main consequences, and perhaps the most enduring legacy, of the Viking presence in England.

6
The burhs of Wessex

King Alfred, late ninth century

At the same time as the growth of these Viking trading settlements, developments in both Wessex and western Mercia were laying the basis for the present-day urban order. Probably during the 880s King Alfred instituted a scheme for the defence of Wessex against Viking attack which involved the construction of a series of burhs at regularly spaced intervals from Kent to Devon. Many if not most of these were non-urban fortresses, though some were fortified towns whose large size and regular layout indicate that (as with the burhs of Offa a century earlier) their military effectiveness was to be maintained by a permanent population. Those on new sites were either large rectilinear constructions on flat land associated with bridges — Cricklade (plate 6), Wallingford and perhaps Wareham — or on elevated spur sites, such as Malmesbury, Lydford and Shaftesbury, while others were laid out in former Roman towns whose defences were reutilised (for instance Exeter, Winchester, Chichester and London). At roughly the same period urban burhs were being founded by Ealdorman Aethelred of Mercia at, for instance, Worcester, Gloucester (fig. 8) and Hereford, a process involving the planned extension of earlier Roman and/or Mercian nuclei. The larger burhs in Wessex were laid out with a rectilinear pattern of defences and streets whose direct inspiration seems to have been the rather smaller rectilinear burhs of late eighth-century Mercia such as Hereford, Northampton, Oxford and Bedford (fig. 5).

The dual character of these places as both military centres and urban foundations is shown by the probably ubiquitous link between the main street system and an intramural or 'wall' street running around the inside of the whole circuit of the defences. This has been recognised at Winchester (fig. 14), London and Canterbury as a new addition to the Roman defences. A 'walkway' at Cricklade (plate 7), 1.2 metres (4 feet) in width and built of flat stones, was probably the first element in the defences to be laid out, before turf for the construction of the bank was stripped from the surrounding area. The defences of these places were also sophisticated: at Cricklade and Lydford a bank and palisade were fronted with a triple ditch system, an arrangement also perhaps detectable at Winchester. As well as being military fortresses these places would also have provided space within the defences for the reception of much of the surrounding population in times of threat, together, no doubt, with many of their animals.

The specifically urban characteristics of these burhs are, however, unmistakable. At Winchester nearly 9 kilometres (5½ miles) of streets were laid out to form a regular grid within the whole of the defended area. Similar grids of streets can be

Plate 6. Cricklade (Wiltshire): a vertical aerial view showing the defences outlined in surrounding field boundaries, and the partly surviving rectilinear layout of the original Saxon town. The river Thames runs from left to right along the top of the photograph. (Photograph: Wiltshire County Council.)

Plate 7. Cricklade (Wiltshire): the intramural walkway (or 'wall street') on the south-west corner of the defences, immediately inside the clay bank (right and top). The loose stones in the centre and left of the picture represent the tumbled remains of a later phase. (Photograph: D. Nicholson.)

recognised in other burhs of this period such as Exeter, Cricklade, Wallingford, Chichester and London. The new streets at Winchester were initially metalled with some 8000 tonnes of flint cobbles (plate 8) and flint beach pebbles were used to surface at least some of the new streets in London, operations which exemplify the sophisticated social arrangements required to construct the burh system as a whole. The street layout at Winchester was associated in the lower lying eastern part of the city with watercourses to be used for fresh water, for industries (such as dyeing and fulling), and to power the city's several mills. The main street and doubtless the side streets as well must have served as the city's market place, though the tendency for urban places to form extramural market areas, already noted in Mercia and apparent in smaller burhs of the tenth century (discussed below), is reflected in the existence of settlement outside the west gate by the late ninth century, and of a market and associated church there by the early tenth century. The creation of the new town also included a church, the New Minster, which by

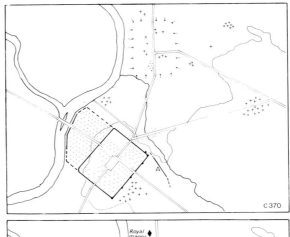

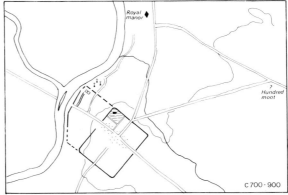

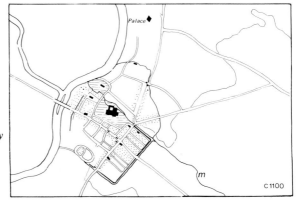

‡⁺‡₊ *burials*

▒▒▒ *known occupied areas*

⊡ *burial chapel or*
    mausoleum

▨▨ *religious precinct*

▬ *church or chapel*

† *ninth and tenth century*
   stone crosses

A *aqueduct*

m *mill*

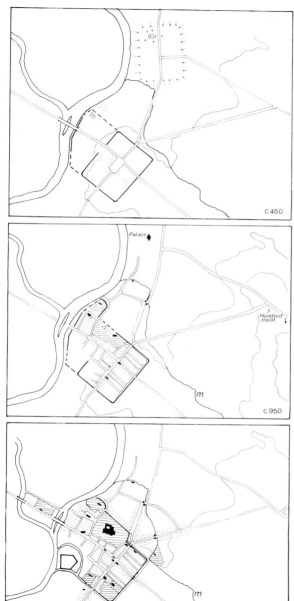

Fig. 8. Gloucester: development phases, showing recolonisation in the tenth and eleventh centuries of the former Roman riverside defended area. (Drawing by Carolyn Heighway.)

Plate 8. Winchester: the flint cobble make-up of the latest Saxon street under the castle, sealed by the depositing of the castle earthwork (top). (Photograph: Winchester Excavations Committee.)

providing for the ecclesiastical and burial needs of the new population was arguably intended to replace the Old Minster. Similar 'New Minsters', probably of the same period, have been found at both Exeter and Gloucester (fig. 8). The provision of new burh churches is discernible in the eighth-century burhs of Mercia and in the later ninth-century burhs of Aethelred in western Mercia such as Gloucester and Cirencester, as well as in the later burhs of Edward the Elder in Wessex and eastern Mercia.

The internal arrangements of late ninth-century Winchester show a marked contrast to the relatively densely packed Viking settlements with elongated properties ranged along streets. The initial settlement of the city was effected, as was that of the other burhs already mentioned, by the parcelling out to lay and ecclesiastical lords of large blocks of land, their subsequent development proceeding by their continuing (and not necessarily regular) division. These tenements may have been associated both for defensive and trading purposes with land holdings near the city, and they can be seen as the origin of the intramural houses dependent upon rural manors which are noted so often in

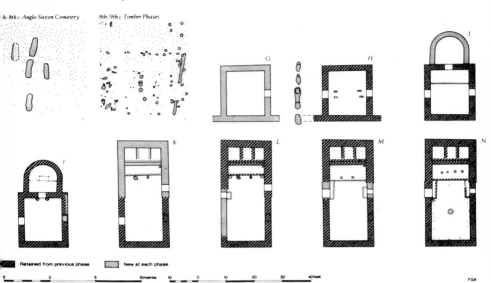

Fig. 9. Winchester: phases of development of St Mary's church, Tanner Street, showing successive stages in the tenth and later centuries from a secular stone structure (phase G, see also fig. 6) of the late eighth and early ninth centuries. (Winchester Excavation Committee.)

Domesday. The changes in the layout of the burh at this time are reflected in the abandonment of the middle Saxon enclosure in Brook Street, mentioned earlier, and the laying out of houses fronting on to a new street traversing the area, the early stone building being transformed in the tenth century into a church (St Mary's) (fig. 9).

Similar processes must have taken place in London, where the 'restoration' of the city by Alfred in 886 resulted in the apportionment of blocks of land, bounded by streets, to individual lords. The description of one of these blocks in a contemporary charter exactly matches the topography of the same area in recent times. London is also one of the few places where archaeological evidence for the use of wharves is forthcoming. A site near the bridge has demonstrated the rebuilding of the remains of the Roman waterfront in probably the early tenth century by the construction of a protective bank and wharves as a communal project (fig. 10).

Edward the Elder

It can be argued that the two decades after the accession of

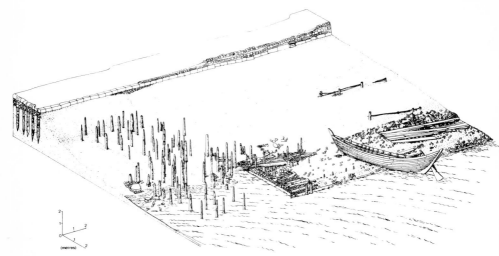

Fig. 10. London: waterfront structures as existing probably in the early to mid tenth century at New Fresh Wharf. Dumps of clay, stone and timber laid up against the remains of the Roman riverside wall provided an embankment for the unloading of boats. (Museum of London.)

Edward the Elder to the throne of Wessex in 899 were one of the most prolific periods of urban foundation and construction in the whole of England between the Roman period and modern times. There is a considerable amount of evidence for the hypothesis that between the years 899 and 911 Edward was responsible for an entirely new defensive strategy for southern England. This appears to have involved the creation of a number of small urban burhs on distinctive topographical sites near river mouths or at estuary heads; these were linked with bridges, both bridge and burh forming a single military unit designed to block rivers against penetration by Viking warships. It can be suggested that this scheme replaced the skeletal and probably incomplete system of fortress burhs initiated by his father Alfred. This policy of Edward's of constructing burh-bridge units to command river access seems to have mirrored that initiated by Offa in Mercia in the late eighth century and is a strategy which also finds many parallels on the continent.

The evidence for this hypothesis is complex, but it explains the numerous instances of small defended burhs in southern England, many of which can be suggested as having replaced more modest non-urban hilltop burhs of possibly Alfredian origin. Two of them (Portchester and Plympton) were built on estates which were newly acquired by Edward, arguably to complete this defensive system.

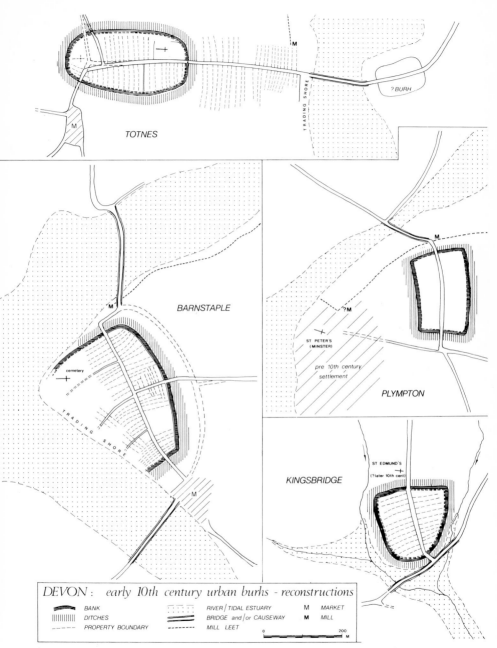

Fig. 11. Devon burhs of the early tenth century: reconstructed topography.

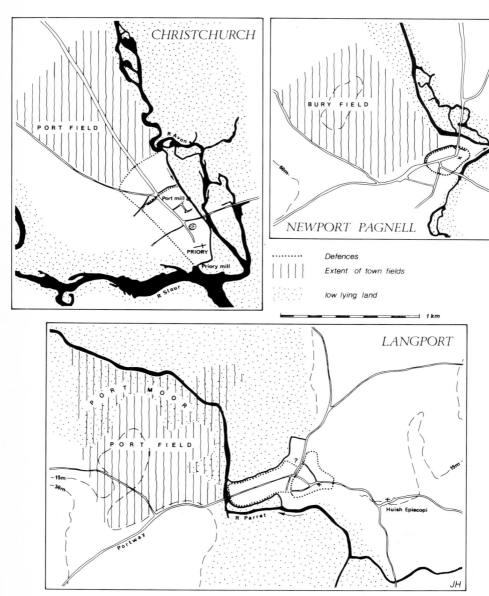

Fig. 12. Early tenth-century burhs at Christchurch (Dorset), Newport Pagnell (Buckinghamshire) and Langport (Somerset), showing the areas of the town fields.

Instances of Alfredian burhs replaced by new urban burhs include Pilton by Barnstaple, Halwell by Totnes and Kingsbridge (fig. 11), Daws Castle by Watchet, Langport (hilltop) by Langport (valley) (fig. 12), *Clausentum* by Southampton, Bredy by Bridport, Burpham by Arundel, and possibly *Eorpeburnan* by New Romney. A number of other estuarine towns probably owe their origin to this phase of systematic burh foundation. Examples include Plympton (now deserted) (fig. 10), Christchurch (fig. 12), Redbridge (Hampshire), Steyning and Pevensey — a list which is by no means complete. There is, furthermore, evidence that several inland burhs were created at this time, some of them again replacing Alfredian fortress burhs. These include Axbridge, Dorchester (Dorset), Wells, Wilton (replacing Old Sarum), Marlborough (fig. 13) (replacing Chisbury), Guildford (replacing Eashing), Newbury and Reading. Some of these (Wells, Marlborough, Wilton and a probably unfortified town at Romsey) appear to have been founded in close association with new high-order ecclesiastical establishments. Many of these places appear to have been new market centres established in a recognisable topographical relationship to early royal estate centres — for instance Axbridge (Somerset) placed on the periphery of an estate centred on the royal and minster site at Cheddar. There is, furthermore, some archaeological evidence that the timber defences of the earlier burhs of Alfred — in particular Cricklade, Wallingford, Wareham and Christchurch — were replaced by stone walls at this period. This complements the systematic provision of new defended urban centres described above and foreshadows similar developments in Mercia.

Some of these places have hitherto been regarded as rather later urban foundations, possibly by Edward's son Athelstan. However, the apparent assurance with which Edward created a similar system of fortified urban centres in the eastern Midlands (described below) as the main instrument in his conquest of the Danelaw after 911 argues that this was a technique which had been tried and tested in southern England in the preceding decade. That these places formed contemporary elements in a single system created by Edward is furthermore suggested by basic similarities in their layout, which can in many cases be paralleled in the layout of Edward's Midland burhs. This general hypothesis is also supported by some recent archaeological evidence, in particular from Southampton. Here, a defended enclosure centred on a single spinal street along the gravel ridge formed the nucleus of the larger medieval town. Dating evidence from the defensive ditch suggests that it was filled up during the reign of Athelstan; other evidence suggests an origin in the years immediately after 900.

As at Southampton, the layout of all these burhs was based upon the pattern of a single main street extending between gates in a defended enclosure, from which irregularly placed side streets ran at right angles. In most cases long narrow properties lined this street, with houses presumably at the street frontages, and extended back to an intramural or 'wall' street running around the inside of the defended perimeter. This linear plan type is merely a scaled-down version of that utilised by King Alfred at Winchester, for instance, and is clearly shown in, for example, the small burhs of Devon (fig. 11). While the contemporaneity of properties, streets and defences cannot be demonstrated unequivocally, the hypothesis that all these features in each burh were the consequence of a single episode of urban foundation appears to explain best all the observed regularities.

There is some evidence that the foundation of all these places was accompanied by the provision of other features which would appear to be necessary accoutrements of a populated urban centre. Most of them have, firstly, a burh church, which might be either an early minster (Christchurch, Wilton, Steyning, Plympton) or else a new church whose parish is often demonstrably secondary to a larger parish or land unit (Kingsbridge, Dorchester, Marlborough [fig. 13]); secondly, many have an adjacent area of land, the 'town fields', designated for use by the burh inhabitants, and often called 'Port Field' in later sources (Christchurch, Langport [fig. 12] and Marlborough [fig. 13]) or 'Bury Fields'; and thirdly, most must have had a mill, in many cases called the 'Port Mill'. Some of these burhs also developed extramural market areas (Barnstaple, Totnes [fig. 11]). All these features were also often associated with the new burhs of both Offa and Alfred. There is good reason to suggest that they were, as with these earlier instances, 'endowments' to the inhabitants on the occasion of the foundation of the burh by the king, as well as being the means whereby the king could retain some measure of economic control over them.

Not all of those burhs suggested as having been created by Edward the Elder in the first decade of the tenth century are mentioned in the Burghal Hidage document. This is an important list of burhs, giving their manning requirements, which has until recently been universally regarded (with an uncritical faith matched only by a disregard of alternative possibilities) as being

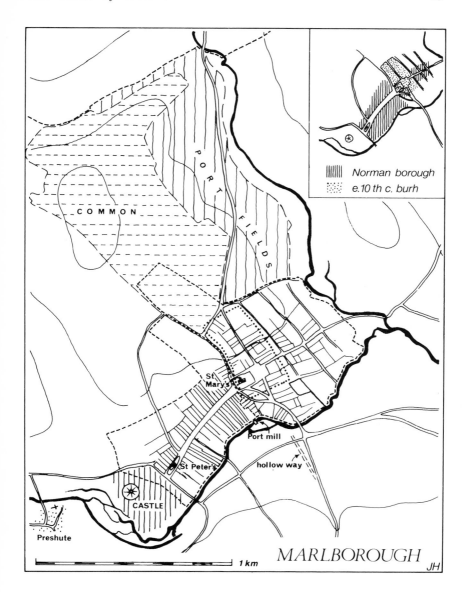

Fig. 13. Marlborough (Wiltshire), showing the early tenth-century burh (St Mary's parish) with the town fields and the early Norman town (St Peter's parish) added on its western side. Both of these settlements are secondary to the earlier village and parish of Preshute.

both of unitary date, around or a little earlier than 919, and a complete (and thus exclusive) catalogue of burhs existing at this date. A recent study has, however, given historical reasons for suggesting that the Burghal Hidage records a state of affairs existing in the late ninth century. This conclusion is considerably strengthened by an examination of the evidence on the ground, which suggests the existence of two different and successive defensive systems. The first was created possibly by Alfred and/or earlier kings, and largely (but not completely) recorded in the Burghal Hidage. This system was at least in part replaced by a new system which was created, it can be inferred, by Edward the Elder before 911.

In the early tenth century, therefore, the urban landscape of a large part at least of southern England consisted on the one hand of distinctive settlements around early royal and ecclesiastical centres, which had arguably been developing truly urban functions by a process of 'organic' growth over a long period. On the other hand, the new burhs of Alfred and Edward comprised an intrusive but dynamic element in the historical landscape. These settlement types were sometimes combined (as at Wells, Wilton, Christchurch and Southampton), but where the burhs were on new sites they formed centres which with few exceptions were to develop steadily as towns in succeeding centuries.

7
The burhs of Mercia

Edward the Elder's reconquest of Mercia from the Danes from 911 was effected by the construction over a period of several years of a series of defended burhs, the size and layout of which demonstrate that they were conceived and built not only as instruments of military conquest but as urban places. It seems likely that this whole campaign was made possible by the security afforded to southern England by the system of urban burhs he had already created around its coasts in the years 899-911. The Mercian burhs share many characteristics with those in the south. They were built on locally inaccessible spur sites though at points of regional accessibility; they were often associated with bridges which probably also had a defensive function; their layout was usually a modified linear form, occasionally rectilinear, and in the later burhs sometimes of modified radial concentric form. The last type often formed a pair with an earlier Mercian and/or Danish burh with a connecting bridge, all three elements combining to form a single military unit preventing passage along the river; examples of these include Southwark, Bedford, Cambridge, Nottingham and Thetford (fig. 5).

At the same time, and probably as part of the same defensive strategy, Aethelred and Edward's sister Aethelflaed were also constructing similar burhs in western Mercia (which include Stafford, Warwick, Shrewsbury, Bridgnorth and Manchester) and refortifying earlier centres such as Worcester, Winchcombe and Tamworth as well as former Roman fortified places such as Chester. There is some evidence to suggest that Bristol, generally thought to be late tenth-century in origin, can be assigned to this stage of burh building. Although its wall can be dated only to the twelfth century, its topography and siting bear striking similarities to other Midland burhs of the late ninth to early tenth century, such as Warwick and Stafford. It seems likely that it was the potentialities of sea trade with Viking towns in Ireland which encouraged the growth at this period of such places as Chester and Gloucester, as well as other towns accessible via the Bristol Channel and Severn estuary such as Barnstaple, Bristol, Worcester and Hereford. Recent research has indeed highlighted the primacy of the riverbank area of Gloucester probably from early in the tenth century (fig. 8). Together these new urban

foundations were (like those in southern England) to lay the basis
for the subsequent development of towns and town life until the
present day.

It is very probable that other burhs were created by Edward,
Aethelred and Aethelflaed besides those mentioned by name in
the Anglo-Saxon Chronicle. These include Oxford, Hereford,
Newport Pagnell, Newport (Essex), probably a number in
Western Mercia (including Coventry) and a whole series of
hitherto unrecognised burhs in eastern England. At Oxford, it
seems likely that the rectangular defences of the Mercian burh
were extended to the west, and possibly also to the east, as new
urban areas — probably at or soon after the start of Edward's
Midland campaign in 911. There is archaeological evidence that
this involved the creation within the enlarged defended enclosure
of a new system of streets, one of which (Church Street)
comprised a laid surface of shaped cobbles extending over the
filled ditch of the earlier Mercian enclosure. A similar extension
to the east of the Mercian enclosure at Hereford can probably be
assigned to this period. At Newport Pagnell (fig. 10) a defended
enclosure on a spur site guarding a bridge, of the same plan type
as the southern English burhs, can probably be identified with the
second unnamed burh built when Edward was staying at
Buckingham in 914. A small burh at Newport in north Essex can
also be identified with a previously unlocated burh built in 917 at
Wigingamere.

There is also much evidence that Edward the Elder built a
series of burhs in eastern England after the capitulation of the
Danish forces in 917. They include Cambridge, Thetford (fig. 6),
Norwich, Bury St Edmunds, Beccles, Sudbury, Woodbridge and
Ipswich, as well as Colchester and Manningtree in Essex. It is
suggested (contrary to prevailing opinion) that these were created
both as secure markets and as a defensive system in depth to
consolidate English gains after this year. At Cambridge the urban
area to the south and east of the river appears to be a new urban
foundation with symmetrically arranged streets and a market
place. With these can be associated defences, described as the
'Kings Ditch', a recanalisation of the river nearer the town
suggesting its creation as an inland port, as well as a mill,
probably a church or churches, and town fields. A burh at
Thetford was built on the northern side of the river around a
probably earlier bridge leading to the Danish settlement on the
southern bank. Although hitherto considered as being of Norman
origin, its D-shaped plan with radial concentric elements bears

Plate 9. Sudbury (Suffolk): a vertical aerial view of the early tenth-century burh. The defences lay inside the curving streets in the centre, enclosing the burh church (top), and with an extramural market place and church (right) outside its gate and another extramural church near the bridge (bottom left). (Photograph: Cambridge University.)

some similarities to those of, for instance, Sudbury (plate 9), Cambridge and Bedford. The defences of Ipswich are also sub-circular in shape and can be associated with a repositioning of the river bridge to perform a new defensive function. These defences would have enclosed the core of the earlier town, though probably left as extramural an area of Viking expansion to the east around St Clement's church. These places would have taken over the functions of earlier Danish settlements as inland ports for North Sea trade.

One major conclusion emerges from this rapid and selective

analysis in particular of the topographical evidence of the layout and siting of these burhs. The great majority of those built by Edward the Elder in both southern and midland England, as well as in southern England and Mercia in the late eighth, ninth and early tenth centuries by others, were created as instruments of a royal fiscal policy, as secure market areas in and by which trading activity could be regulated and controlled by the king both for the public good and to increase the power and influence of the king. The defensive and market functions of these places were contemporary and complementary, both (as it turned out) serving to ensure their long-term survival.

8
The later tenth century

During succeeding decades, however, purely geographical or economic forces played their part in the development of these urban burhs. Although the limits of settlement or the degree of urbanisation in these places at any particular period can seldom be determined, all the evidence suggests a steady if not rapid growth of all these places through the tenth century, reflecting such factors as a climatic optimum at this time, the development of trading networks already perhaps established by the Vikings, the development of coinage and the establishment of mints in towns under the strong late Saxon kings, and the attempts by successive kings to limit trading to such towns by legislation. These towns became legal, administrative, trading and industrial centres: there is, for example, evidence from many towns for the development of pottery making as an urban-based industry. Production in the tenth century of generally high-class wares destined for regional distribution has so far been recognised at York, Torksey, Lincoln, Stamford, Nottingham, Chester, Norwich, Thetford, Leicester, Northampton, Stafford, Gloucester, Winchester, Cricklade, Bath and Exeter — probably by no means an exhaustive list.

The internal expansion of many of these burhs in the tenth century has in some cases been demonstrated archaeologically. The developments in tenth-century York have already been referred to. Colonisation of the defended area of Winchester was virtually complete by the end of the century, with the development of probably most of the streets by houses set gable-end to the street, the concentration of single trades in discrete areas of the town, and the development of industries such as pottery and tile making, bell-founding and the working of gold, silver, bronze and iron, as well as bone and ivory. Some of this expansion was furthermore reflected in the growth of 'suburbs' outside most of the principal gates. The build-up of at least eight layers of cobbling and earth on one of the peripheral streets sealed under the Norman castle demonstrates the extent to which widespread occupation within the walls necessitated the constant repair of these streets before the Norman Conquest (plate 8). A similar accretion of layers of earth and gravel at an early date has also been demonstrated on streets at Oxford. An expansion of settlement within the original defences in the tenth century can also be discerned from archaeological evidence from such places as Warwick and Wareham.

There is little if any evidence after about 920 of the creation of urban burhs as royal foundations on the pattern of those created by Edward the Elder. On the contrary, there is some indication that in the middle of the century, when the likelihood of Viking attack had receded, the maintenance of the defences of some, possibly many, burhs was allowed to lapse. This can be demonstrated at Cricklade; and at Southampton the ditch of the seaward defences was deliberately filled in the second quarter of the century. It is possibly to this period that the growth of settlement around extramural market places of burhs in both southern and midland England (e.g. Barnstaple, Totnes, Malmesbury, Shaftesbury, Sudbury [plates 9], Maldon and Newport [Essex]) can be assigned. At Shaftesbury such a shift of settlement to the market area outside the original defences could well have led at an early date to the virtual abandonment of the late ninth-century burh.

The general process of urban growth in the tenth century was also manifested in a new phenomenon: that of the foundation by monastic establishments of towns outside their gates as speculative ventures. These include Peterborough, Whitby, Hartlepool and Durham; similar developments can be inferred from topographical evidence at (for instance) Ely, Glastonbury and Tavistock. These new foundations generally consisted of triangular market places lined with burgage plots outside the main abbey gate. A similar development occurred, though arguably in the early tenth century, at Romsey (about 907), and a later development of similar type can be recognised at Coventry, where a market was arguably established outside a newly created priory in 1043. This process continued at Battle, where a new abbey and town were established between 1066 and 1071.

The new phase of Viking raiding in the early eleventh century affected towns in various ways. Several hillforts, such as South Cadbury and Old Sarum, were redefended and local mints transferred to them. There is some evidence that these places were designed to be more than temporary refuges, belying their description as 'emergency burhs', although the defensive measures were piecemeal rather than systematic. Minting continued through the eleventh century at, for instance, Old Sarum, though the move of moneyers there from nearby Wilton in about 1003 probably involved a shift only of the royal administrative centre, rather than of any of the latter's 'urban' functions.

There are indications that Cnut encouraged the well-being of towns whose defences had earlier been refurbished against his depredations. However, evidence from Cricklade has shown that the stone wall surrounding the burh was deliberately razed to the ground and the defensive ditches filled with stones, arguably by Cnut soon after 1016. Similar evidence can be recognised at Wareham, Lydford, Christchurch and South Cadbury. Nevertheless, minting continued at Cricklade, and the 'emergency' mint at Old Sarum was augmented by new moneyers at Wilton, and that at South Cadbury entirely replaced by the same moneyers setting up at lowland sites at Ilchester, Bruton and Crewkerne. The same relationship can be found between the hillfort at Cissbury and Chichester, and between *Eanbyri* (an unknown fort, but possibly Maiden Castle) and Dorchester (Dorset). These considerations and the presence of Cnut's palace at Winchester suggest that he was aware of the importance of urban communities in the economic life of the kingdom he had attained. This important role was to continue for the rest of the 'Anglo-Saxon' period until the Norman Conquest.

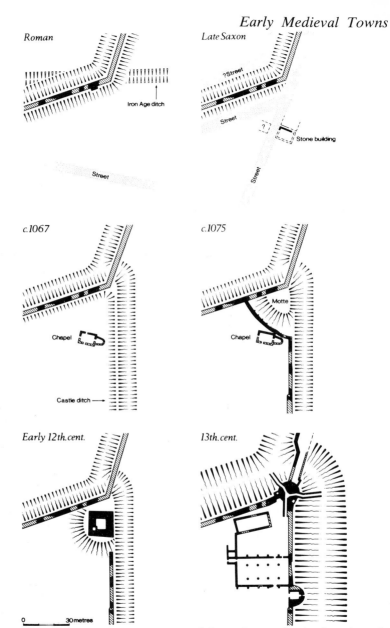

Fig. 14. Winchester: phases of development of the castle area showing how the early Norman castle has obliterated intramural and extramural Saxon streets and buildings. (Winchester Excavation Committee.)

9
Norman towns

The changing political circumstances caused by the Norman Conquest in 1066 were responsible in the short as well as the long term for some fundamental changes to both urban life and the urban landscape. Though the new regime caused perhaps few changes to the general level of urban material culture, towns were political as well as social organisms, and overall changes to their fabric in the first few years after the Conquest reflected the changed political order. The most immediate effects of the Conquest on the fabric of the townscape were twofold: firstly, the imposition of castles on to the existing urban layout, and secondly, the removal of many cathedrals to larger towns from smaller settlements. A second major consequence of the Norman presence was the relatively rapid growth of towns in the century after 1066, which reflected political and military realities, a steadily increasing population and the introduction of new trading patterns. These developments resulted in firstly the planned extension of some of the earlier Saxon centres outside their original defences, and secondly the creation of towns on new sites, often close to new castles.

Castles and cathedrals

The history and physical development of Norman and later castles has been much studied, but the relationship of these to the townscapes into which they were intruded has been relatively ignored. There is little doubt that the destruction caused by their imposition on to generally thriving urban places was considerable, and the number of houses lost to this process is frequently recorded in Domesday Book. As well as buildings, however, it is clear from topographical and some archaeological evidence that in some cases whole streets and even churches were obliterated, causing drastic modifications to the townscape.

Examples of these processes can be seen in the present-day topography of almost every large Saxon burh in which a Norman castle was placed (figs. 5 and 7). The construction of the castle at Winchester, built within one corner of the walled space (fig. 14), involved the destruction of a whole length of street lined with buildings, a length of intramural or wall street and a similar length of an extramural street also lined with buildings. Furthermore, the extension of the royal palace in about 1070 also involved the destruction of part of the centre of the town, including several streets, houses and part of the cemetery of the New Minister. Similarly, castles at Cambridge and Oxford probably destroyed whole streets, as well as at Cambridge the main burh and early minster church of St Giles and its graveyard. There are indications that the construction of the Tower of London probably necessitated the obliteration of one of the gates through the city walls and the consequent reorganisation of the streets both inside and outside the defences.

Many similar instances can be given. In some cases, however, pre-Conquest churches survived within the castle precincts, retaining their earlier parochial and/or burial rights; these have been recognised at, among others, Oxford, Dover, Hastings, Pevensey, Leicester, Warwick and possibly Old Sarum. The church of St Peter ad Vincula at the Tower of London is probably a similar case, having originally had burial rights and a parish which comprised an area both inside and outside the suggested earlier gateway.

The transference of a number of cathedrals to central urban locations and the rebuilding of Saxon cathedral minsters (for instance, Exeter and Winchester) were another Norman innovation which in some cases caused further disruption to earlier urban patterns. The relocation of cathedrals from Dorchester (Oxfordshire) to Lincoln and from Thetford to Norwich are two examples. At Norwich almost the whole of the area of the burh to the south of the river was requisitioned for the new cathedral and priory precinct, necessitating the destruction of several streets, doubtless many houses, and at least two churches.

New Norman towns

While these developments may in some cases have caused devastating changes to the fabric of many towns, it was the creation of new towns by the Normans which was to effect the greatest change to the old urban order. These either formed additions, many of them planned, to existing centres or were new foundations on fresh sites.

The addition of new 'suburbs' to earlier towns in the half century or so after the Conquest caused considerable changes to many towns, both large and small. Often the new areas took the form of simple additions, on the side of the town nearest the castle, of a single block of properties along a wide street, which in many cases would have formed a new market. Such areas can be observed for instance at Lincoln, Bristol or Marlborough. In Marlborough, for example (fig. 13), a wide new street was laid out between the early Norman castle (built on a prehistoric mound) and the Saxon burh to the east, probably during the 1070s or 1080s, and was provided with a new church, whose small parish encompassed this new urban area. Probably as the direct result of the concentration there of Norman legal and administrative functions, which included the transference of the mint from nearby Great Bedwyn in 1068, this new town became one of the earliest centres for industrialised cloth weaving and fulling in the West Country.

On a more dramatic scale, additions to earlier Saxon centres sometimes took the form of large planned extensions which were in effect new towns, with their own parochial provisions, markets and legal and commercial customs. Examples of such large foundations can be recognised at Nottingham and Norwich. In the former case a new town was laid out between the castle and the Saxon burh around a large market place of pre-Conquest origin. In the case of Norwich new streets and a market were laid out on a rectilinear module to the west of the Saxon nucleus, probably at least in part the consequence of the displacement of population resulting from the imposition of the new Norman cathedral and castle in this area.

A further example can be seen at Bury St Edmunds, where a large new town, again of rectilinear plan, was added by the abbot probably in the 1070s (or possibly rather earlier) to the earlier defended late Saxon nucleus and monastic precinct, dwarfing the Saxon town in scale. The Saxon burh at Southampton was also enlarged with the addition of new streets, with the building of a castle there in the later twelfth century (though which came first, the enlarged town or the castle, is a matter for debate); the new streets formed a rectilinear grid around the castle. At Nottingham, Norwich and Southampton these new areas were divided into French and English boroughs, each with its different customs.

The new towns of the Norman period on fresh sites are of many different types. Some forty-seven new towns were founded in England in the period 1066-1140, and about twenty in Wales, the majority of them attached to and in many cases intimately connected with a royal or baronial castle. This was especially so in Wales and the counties bordering it (the Marches), where by 1087 the Marcher Lords had created several castles with associated boroughs (for instance Wigmore, Clifford, Chepstow, Montgomery, Caernarfon and Cardiff). In large measure this programme of town building carried across the Channel a practice that had already been common in Normandy before the Conquest.

Although castles were undoubtedly powerful stimuli to urban growth on new sites as well as at established centres, the assumption that the presence of a town was the consequence, rather than the cause, of the construction of a castle on a site should not be too hastily made. For example, at Thetford (fig. 5) and Arundel, commonly regarded as new Norman 'castle towns', there are grounds for suggesting the existence at these places of tenth-century urban burhs to which the castle came late in the process of urban development. At Old Sarum, on the other hand, it now seems likely that the siting there of the Norman castle and cathedral was the consequence not of the existence of a pre-Conquest urban place but only of the presence of a royal administrative centre of early eleventh-century origin. Its development as an urban place was in this case clearly a consequence of these developments in the Norman period.

The variations shown by these places, both in plan and in scale, are wide, and they range from large foundations such as Ludlow to relatively small ones such as Devizes. Many of these incorporated a market and a parish church, although in other cases the streets or shoreline (as at Rye or Shoreham) were used as the market areas. In most instances the market place, forming a dominant feature of the town, was focused on the castle. At Ludlow the market lies along the ridge opposite the castle gate, and at Devizes (fig. 15) the market lay astride the original way leading from the main castle entrance to the earlier village to the east. In other instances, where the town was not directly associated with a castle, the market place still provided the dominant focus for the town, as at St Ives (Cambridgeshire), Lichfield or Bury St Edmunds. At St Ives, founded by the Abbot of Ramsey in about 1110, the new town was laid out around an elongated market area near the river. At the same time the roadway to the earlier village to the west was diverted over a new causeway and bridge across the river and its valley, in precisely the same way (though for dissimilar reasons) as were many of the burhs of Edward the Elder two centuries earlier. The market at Battle, laid out outside the abbey gates, continued a tradition of development begun in the tenth century.

One of the most interesting variations of layout is shown by new urban foundations which occupied in effect the outer ward or

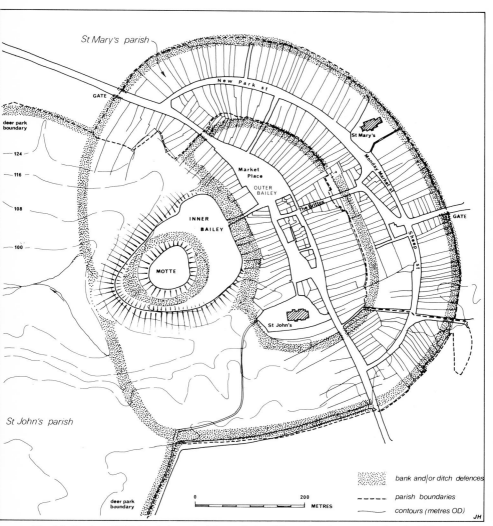

Fig. 15. Devizes (Wiltshire): layout of the early twelfth-century town around and within a castle and its baileys (St Mary's parish), with subsequent colonisation of the former bailey by a new market in the mid to late twelfth century.

bailey of the castle, both having common defences. Examples of this form can be seen at Devizes, Lauceston, Wisbech and Tutbury, where the internal streets mirror to a large extent the shape of the outer castle defences, or Pontefract, Cardiff and Pembroke, where the outer town and castle defences enclose a single spinal street. Devizes, built in the early twelfth century, is a good example of this type (fig. 15). The original urban area consisted of a wide curved street with its own market and church (as with Marlborough, its parish coterminous with the new urban area), laid out around the main (second) bailey. The bank and ditch defences of this outer urban ward or third bailey formed a single unit with the bank and ditch of a large deer park on the other side of the castle. A second phase of urban expansion around a large elongated market place later colonised the second bailey probably in the middle of the century, a development which mirrors in a curiously inverse way the growth of an additional market area at Pontefract *outside* the gate of the original defended nucleus. Both places were founded in close proximity to earlier villages whose layout is still discernible in the present-day topography. In these, as in other examples, the castles and the original towns with their common defences formed separate but closely linked areas which were complementary in function.

Not all the new Norman towns were defended as a matter of course. The defended seigneurial boroughs attached to castles of the later eleventh century in the Marches have an obvious but local defensive role, and at Devizes at least the town, its defences and the castle defences are all contemporary with the reconstruction of the castle by Bishop Roger in the early twelfth century. But the extensive urban expansions of the eleventh and early twelfth centuries (at Nottingham and Southampton for instance) were not provided with defences until the mid and later twelfth century, and that at Norwich not until the mid thirteenth century. Furthermore the defences of the castle town of Ludlow are now thought to be additions to a larger unwalled town, in places cutting across existing properties and boundaries. The undefended towns, at St Ives (about 1110) and Lichfield, laid out in a grid plan in the second quarter of the twelfth century, have already been mentioned.

It is clear even from the few examples quoted that the Normans created a new economic and political climate in which towns, both old and new, played an important role. Unlike those of the Saxon burhs, the new defences of both castle and town, though they were (especially before 1100) instruments of central government, were constructed not as communal defended centres for the whole population but rather as fortresses for the protection of the ruling classes and for the control of newly captured territory. In the twelfth century, however, urban foundations created by seigneurial lords as speculative ventures became more common and were usually sited to take advantage of the geographical and economic rather than the defensive potential of new sites. Many new castle towns were founded in this century with these aims, but increasingly the existence of a castle and the concentration of administrative and legal functions at a particular place became less important factors in either the security or the success of towns. In some cases purely economic inducements led to the growth of settlement around originally extramural market areas of pre-Conquest origin, such as those at Bedford, Hereford, Stamford, Nottingham, Northampton and London, though such developments must in most cases have been a continuation of 'suburban' settlement growth begun in the tenth century if not earlier. At Hereford and Northampton, as at Winchester, these suburbs were provided with their own defences (though at precisely what period is not known), reflecting similar but more pronounced developments on the continent.

The growth of coastal rather than inland ports at this period is a further manifestation of these tendencies. The concentration of royal administrative functions at Winchester in the late Saxon and early Norman periods was a major factor in the success of the town in these periods, but the demise of these functions led to a decline of the town's prosperity after the mid twelfth century and a corresponding growth of the port of Southampton. Similar shifts of economic focus can be seen between Norwich, an important early Norman administrative centre and port, and Great Yarmouth, between Lincoln and Boston, and between Steyning and New Shoreham. A further example is King's Lynn, which originated in the foundation of a market and settlement in the late eleventh century. This grew (doubtless beyond the founder's expectations) by successive stages in the twelfth and thirteenth centuries to become a major seaport, which at an early stage took over many of the functions of former inland ports such as Cambridge and Thetford and, at a later period, Wisbech.

The internal layout of the new towns of the Norman period has not been studied systematically, but many of the plan types were doubtless developed to accommodate the long narrow burgage plots into which the internal spaces were divided. These could best have been arranged along a linear or 'high street' plan, rather than in an evenly rectilinear arrangement of streets, and this must account for the ubiquity of the former type. Inferences can sometimes be drawn from topographical indications for the internal development of the townscape: at Marlborough the different widths and lengths of plots along the eleventh-century High Street suggest its development over a period of time. On the other hand, the existence of supposedly discrete plan elements at Ludlow are now thought not to indicate different phases of its growth. There is some indication that burgage plot widths were related to standard sizes of timber buildings, which were placed with either their gable-ends or (less commonly) long sides to the street. With only a few exceptions the buildings were of timber-framed construction, built up to the street frontage, until stone buildings became more common from the later twelfth century onwards. There is, however, both documentary and archaeological evidence from Winchester suggesting that domestic two-storeyed structures of masonry belonging to the higher ranks of society, their ground storeys consisting of probably barrel-vaulted undercrofts used as shops or storehouses, may well have had an origin in the later Saxon period. The universal use (as in earlier periods) of cess and latrine pits, in addition to wells, in the back gardens of individual plots is well evidenced from excavated sites. Public water supplies and rubbish disposal facilities were still a thing of the future.

The development of the pattern of urban churches and parishes was in most towns complete by the mid twelfth century, if not rather earlier in some towns. Many of the smaller Norman towns were, like the Wessex and Mercian burhs of two centuries earlier, provided with their own churches, their parishes carved out of earlier units. This is particularly clear at Marlborough and Devizes, discussed earlier (figs. 13 and 15). In the larger towns of Saxon origin the area served by the urban or pre-urban minster was, it seems, gradually carved up by the foundation of churches whose small, mainly intramural parishes served single 'estates' within the town, the churches being built and owned by the estate owner. In Norwich, and probably in other places such as London, Winchester and Exeter, these processes appear to have led to a steady growth in the number of churches from the tenth century to the mid twelfth, when the pattern was probably complete, reflecting both the expansion and the internal colonisation of these towns during this period.

The developments in the urban landscape during the Norman

period described in this chapter provided both the physical and the economic framework for later developments; it is possible to recognise in them the development of many of the economic tendencies which were to lead to further growth during the succeeding two centuries of the medieval period.

10
Further reading

Aston, M., and Bond J. *The Landscape of Towns.* J. M. Dent, 1976. Some useful topographical material, and summary discussion of urban development.

Barley, M. W. (editor). *European Towns — Their Archaeology and Early History.* Academic Press/CBA, 1977. An indispensible source.

Biddle, M. (editor). *Winchester in the Early Middle Ages.* Clarendon Press, 1976. A model for the discussion of early urban development.

Brooke, C., and Keir, G. *London 800-1216: The Shaping of a City.* Secker and Warburg, 1975. Synthesis of historical and some topographical material.

Haslam, J. (editor). *Anglo-Saxon Towns in Southern England.* Phillimore, 1984. General surveys by county.

Maitland, W. *Township and Borough.* Cambridge University Press, 1898. Includes much valuable discussion.

Platt, C. *The English Medieval Town.* Secker and Warburg, 1976. A general history, but sketchy on the early period.

Reynolds, S. *English Medieval Towns.* Clarendon Press, 1977. Cast in the same mould as Tait's book (below); useful bibliography.

Soulsby, I. *The Towns of Medieval Wales.* Phillimore, 1983. Discussion and gazetteer.

Stephenson, J. *Borough and Town, A Study of Urban Origins.* Medieval Academy of America, 1933. Useful discussion and synthesis, but denies existence of Saxon towns.

Tait, J. *The Medieval English Borough.* Manchester University Press, 1936, reprinted 1968. A reply to Stephenson's one-sided arguments.

Most of these books contain substantial bibliographies of books and articles both of general interest and relating to particular towns.

Index